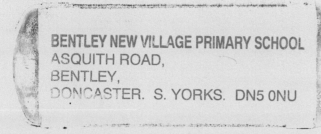

How have things changed?

At Home

James Nixon

W

FRANKLIN WATTS

LONDON • SYDNEY

This edition published in 2012 by
Franklin Watts
338 Euston Road
London NW1 3BH

Franklin Watts Australia
Level 17/207 Kent Street
Sydney NSW 2000

ISBN: 978 1 4451 0791 2

Dewey classification number: 643

A CIP catalogue record for this book is available
from the British Library.

Planning and production by Discovery Books Limited
Editor: James Nixon
Designer: Rob Norridge

Photographs: p6 (top) Chesterfield Museum Service and www.picturethepast.org.uk, p6 (bottom)
Getty Images, p7 (top) Bobby Humphrey, p7 (bottom) Lisa Turay/istockphoto.com, p8 (top) Weald and
Downland Open Air Museum, p8 (middle) Bobby Humphrey, p8 (bottom) Chris Fairclough, p9 (top)
Chris Fairclough, p9 (bottom) Bobby Humphrey, p10 (top) Mary Evans Picture Library, p10 (bottom)
Chris Fairclough, p11 (top) Staffordshire Arts and Museum Service, p11 (bottom) Bobby Humphrey,
p12 (left) Tsu Shi Weng/istockphoto.com, p12 (right) Bob Randall/istockphoto.com, p12 (bottom)
Mary Evans Picture Library, p13 (top) Rafik El Raheb/istockphoto.com, p13 (middle) Bobby
Humphrey, p13 (bottom) Richard Schmidt-Zuper/istockphoto.com, p14 (top) Nottingham County
Council and www.picturethepast.org.uk, p14 (bottom) Bobby Humphrey, p15 Bobby Humphrey, p16
(top) Getty Images, p16 (bottom) Nottingham County Council and www.picturethepast.org.uk, p17
(top) David Hughes/istockphoto.com, p17 (middle) Slobo Mitic/istockphoto.com, p17 (bottom) Robin
Akin/istockphoto.com, p18 (top) Getty Images, p18 (bottom) Getty Images, p19 Bobby Humphrey,
p20 (top) Mary Evans Picture Library, p20 (bottom) istockphoto.com, p21 Bobby Humphrey, p22 Mary
Evans Picture Library, p23 (top) Bobby Humphrey, p23 (bottom) Chris Fairclough, p24 The Advertising
Archives, p25 Bobby Humphrey, p26 Mary Evans Picture Library, p27 (top) Beamish Open Air
Museum, p27 (bottom) Bobby Humphrey.

Cover photos: (top) Beamish Open Air Museum, (bottom) Bobby Humphrey.

Printed in China

Franklin Watts is a division of Hachette Children's Books,
an Hachette UK company
www.hachette.co.uk

Contents

What kind of home do you live in? What materials were used to build your home? Do you know how old it is?

Then and now

Look at the pictures of the street then and now. How many differences can you spot?

1950s

1955

Most homes are a lot older than you are. These houses were built in the 1950s. How many different families do you think have lived in one of these houses since then?

This picture of a living room shows how the inside of a home looked in the 1950s.

Homes and life in the home have changed a lot over the years. Look at the houses built in the 1950s today. They have new doors and windows. Many of the houses now have a satellite dish on the wall.

Now

The insides of houses have changed a lot, too. Look at this modern living room. The style of the furniture and **decoration** is very different from the 1950s.

Now

Then and now

Do you like the old or new living room? Make a list of your reasons.

7

The building

In **medieval** times the homes of most people were small and simple.

The buildings had **timber** frames. The thatched roof had a hole in the top for a chimney. Floors were covered with straw. Windows did not have glass. They were just openings that were covered with wooden shutters.

By **Tudor** times houses had chimneys, but they still had timber frames.

By **Victorian** times homes were built of brick like this one.

Today, the homes of ordinary people are often a lot bigger than they were in the past.

What kind of home would you prefer to live in and why?

The most common building material in modern homes is brick, but other materials are used, such as timber or **concrete**. Some houses are joined together. Others are **detached** like the homes in the picture above.

In a block of flats homes are built on top of one another.

How do people reach the flats at the top of a tall block?

9

Changing homes

During Victorian times thousands of factory workers lived in areas of poor housing called slums.

In the slums, tiny houses were built close together in long rows called **terraces**.

1950

Each house had a toilet in a small yard. This picture of '**back-to-backs**' from the 1950s was taken just before they were knocked down. Many slums were demolished around this time.

Now

Some Victorian terraced houses do remain today, but they have been **modernised**. They now have inside toilets. Many of the houses in this photo have had extra rooms added in the roof.

Wealthy Victorians did not want to be close to the dirty slums in the city centres. Some very wealthy people lived on country **estates** like this one called Shugborough Hall.

1870

Now

This is Shugborough!

The Complete Working
SHUGBOROUGH
Historic Estate

The nation's most complete, working historic estate.
Open every day from mid-March to end October

A lot of the large country houses have been turned into hotels or **tourist attractions**. Look at Shugborough Hall today. It doesn't look very different, but it is now run by the **National Trust**. The public pay to visit the house.

There was no electricity in most Victorian homes.

In the evenings people lit their homes with oil lamps like this one.

People went upstairs to bed by candlelight. Imagine how dark and spooky this would be!

Before electricity, housework was a lot more difficult. Many of the machines we use today had not been invented. Look at this picture taken in 1905 of one of the first vacuum cleaners. They were huge machines that were carried from door to door on a horse and cart.

How is this machine sucking up dust from the rooms above the shop?

Since the 1930s most homes have had electricity. At the flick of a switch you can light up a dark room.

What electrical items can you see in this photo?

Now

Electricity has changed the way we live. Has your home ever had its power cut? Think of the things you can't do when there is a power cut.

Today, people can get electricity in different ways. The **solar panels** on the roof of this house convert the sun's energy into electricity.

The main feature of a Victorian kitchen was the **range**. Ranges were still common in kitchens in the 1950s.

Part of the range was a wood or coal burning stove. This provided the heat to cook food and warm water.

1950

How is the warmth of the range being used in this picture?

There were few **appliances** and they were usually worked by hand like this mincer. The kitchen was an important part of family life. The warmth of the range made the kitchen a good place to eat and relax.

Now

Most kitchens today do not have a range. Look at this modern kitchen. It has lots of cupboards and drawers for storage. An electric cooker, a microwave, a dishwasher and a fridge are built into the cupboards.

How does the kitchen in your home compare to the ones in the pictures?

Electrical appliances, like toasters and kettles, make work in the kitchen quick and easy. Foods can be chopped or mixed quickly in food processors like this one.

The bathroom

Not many families could afford homes with bathrooms in the 1930s.

This baby is being washed in a small tin tub in the kitchen.

1933

1460·38

People often had their baths in front of the warm range. The water was collected from an outside pump and heated on the stove. Even by the 1950s some homes did not have a bathroom.

1950

How would you like to have a bath in your living room?

Here is a modern-day bathroom. You can choose to wash in a big bath or have a shower. Today, hot water comes straight from the taps.

Then and now

Do you think bathtime was better in the past or now? Why?

Soap

In early Victorian, times soap was too expensive for poor people. It was a **luxury** that was **taxed**. Once people realised that soap was needed to help kill germs the tax was stopped and soap began to be mass-produced. Today, everybody uses soap.

The bedroom

Most houses in the 1940s were smaller than they are today. They often had only one or two bedrooms.

Look at this young girl's bedroom in 1944. How can you tell that she had to share the room with her baby sister or brother?

1944

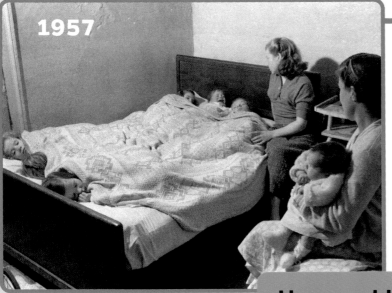

1957

Families also tended to be larger at this time. In this photo six children are crammed into one bedroom. They have to share a bed together and sleep head to toe.

How would you feel if you had to share a bed with your brothers and sisters?

Families today are often smaller than in the past. A lot of children have their own bedroom.

Children had fewer toys in the past so bedrooms often looked a lot barer than they do today.

Now

Then and now

In your room you may have your own television, stereo, or even a personal computer. This boy is playing computer games.

What things can you spot in this bedroom that you would not find in a bedroom a hundred years ago?

Doing the washing

There were no washing machines over a hundred years ago. The laundry was washed by hand.

Clothes were soaked in a tub of soapy water. A wooden tool called a dolly was then used to loosen the dirt.

1890

After washing, clothes were put through a mangle like this one to squeeze out the water. Doing the laundry took all day.

The invention of the washing machine, tumble dryer and electric iron made housework a lot easier. Washing and drying is just a matter of filling and emptying the machines. Doing this only takes a few minutes.

Now

Irons

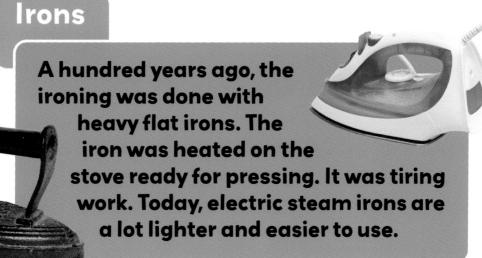

A hundred years ago, the ironing was done with heavy flat irons. The iron was heated on the stove ready for pressing. It was tiring work. Today, electric steam irons are a lot lighter and easier to use.

Meals

In the 1930s meals were nearly always homemade. Housewives spent a lot of their time cooking.

1930

Bread and cakes were usually baked at home as well. This was cheaper than buying ready-made goods from a shop. Most families could not afford to eat out in restaurants.

Today, many people still cook their own meals and bake their own cakes. But it is also common for people to buy ready meals from the shops. These meals often only need heating and can be ready in minutes.

Cakes and biscuits are usually bought in packets as well.

Nowadays many families often choose to eat out or order a **takeaway**.

Over fifty years ago the housework took such a long time as there were fewer machines to help.

Women rarely worked outside the home. Their job was to look after the family and the home while the men went out to work.

Look at this advert from 1946 for a cleaning product. It was aimed at women because they usually did the housework.

Today, there are many more machines to help with the housework. It takes much less time. More and more women are choosing to go out to work.

Who does the housework in your family?

Men do more housework and **chores** than they did in the past. This man is doing the ironing and the washing up.

Do you help with any of the chores?

Home entertainment

Around ninety years ago families had to make their own entertainment.

They talked, read stories or sang songs together. Many families had a piano in the house and would listen to someone playing and sing along. This picture from 1919 shows children listening to their mother playing the piano.

1919

How many children does the mother in this picture have?

Look at these people reading in their living room in 1961. Even fifty years ago there was a lot less to do than there is today. Some homes still did not have a television.

1961

Nowadays there are more things to entertain us in the home. This family are watching a film on their television using a DVD player.

Pets

Pets are more common than they were a hundred years ago. Can you spot the family pet in this photo? Look back at the photos on page 16 and see if you can find a pet that was popular in the 1950s.

Now

Glossary

Appliances Pieces of equipment used to perform tasks in the home.

Back-to-backs Terraced houses that backed on to another row of houses.

Chores Household tasks.

Concrete A heavy building material made from a mixture of sand, cement and broken stone.

Decoration The type of paint or wallpaper in a room.

Detached Describes a house that is not joined to any other.

Estates Big areas of land in the country, with a large house, owned by one family.

Luxury An item that people enjoy very much, but do not often have as it is expensive.

Medieval Relating to the period of history from 1000 to 1453.

Modernised Made more modern or up-to-date.

National Trust An organisation that looks after places of historic interest.

Range A large cooking stove with a hob and one or more ovens, that was kept continuously hot to heat the house.

Solar panels Thin layers of a special material that are fixed in a place where they can take in energy from the Sun.

Takeaway A meal picked up from a restaurant.

Taxed Describes something you buy where a certain amount of the price is paid to the government.

Terraces Rows of houses joined together.

Timber Wood that has been prepared for use in building.

Tourist attractions Places that are visited for pleasure.

Tudor Relating to the reign of the Tudor kings and queens, which lasted from from 1453 to 1603.

Victorian Relating to the reign of Queen Victoria, which lasted from 1837 to 1901.

Further information

Places to visit:

Beamish Open Air Museum, County Durham (www.beamish.org.uk)
This award-winning museum has a wide collection of fully-furnished homes from the 1800s and 1900s.

St Fagans National History Museum, Cardiff
(www.museumwales.ac.uk/en/stfagans/)
St Fagans explores how the people of Wales have lived through the ages.

Weald and Downland Open Air Museum, Sussex (www.wealddown.co.uk)
Here you can wander around the collection of nearly 50 different homes from the last 500 years.

Portsmouth City Museum (www.portsmouthcitymuseums.co.uk)
Discover how life in the home has changed over the centuries in the reconstructed homes in this museum.

Websites:

www.bbc.co.uk/education/dynamo/history/stepback.htm
steps back in time to see life in the home in 1900

www.ngfl-cymru.org.uk/vtc/kitchen_past_present/eng/Introduction
compares kitchens in the past to today

www.woodlands-junior.kent.sch.uk/Homework/houses.html
looks at the different buildings used for homes through history

Books to read:

At Home (A Victorian Childhood), Ruth Thomson, 2007 (Franklin Watts)
In the Home (History from Photographs), Kathleen Cox and Pat Hughes, 2006 (Wayland)
Home Sweet Home (Changes), Liz Gogerly, 2006 (Wayland)
Homes (History Snapshots), Sarah Ridley, 2007 (Franklin Watts)
Houses and Homes (History from Photographs) Kathleen Cox and Pat Hughes, 2006, (Wayland)
Houses and Homes (Where You Live), Ruth Nason, 2007 (Franklin Watts)
Victorian Homes (Life in the Past), Mandy Ross, 2005 (Heinemann)

Index